101 TIPS FOR A GREAT MARRIAGE

101 tips for a good, solid, exciting, spicy, enjoyable, creative, loving, innovative, happy, joyful, lasting, emulative, fulfilling and exemplary marriage.

Michael & Bernice Hutton-Wood

HWP

Unless otherwise indicated, all scriptural references are taken from the King James Version of the Bible.

101 TIPS FOR A GREAT MARRIAGE

101 tips for a good, solid, exciting, spicy, enjoyable, creative, loving, innovative, happy, joyful, lasting, emulative, fulfilling and exemplary marriage.

ISBN 978-0-9562541-5-3

Copyright © MAY 2011 by Michael Hutton-Wood

Hutton-Wood publications

In the UK write to:
Michael Hutton-Wood Ministries
P. O. Box 1226, Croydon. CR9 6DG.

Or in the UK

Call: Tel. 020 8689 6010; 07956 815 714

Outside the UK call: +44 20 8689 6010; +44 7956 815 714

Or contact:
WEBSITE: www.houseofjudah.org.uk
Email: michaelhutton-wood@fsmail.net
houseofjudah@ymail.com
leadersfactoryinternational@yahoo.com

Published & distributed by: Michael Hutton-Wood Ministries
(Incorporating Hutton-Wood World Outreach Ministries)

Printed in the United Kingdom

hwp

THE MANDATE

'...SET IN ORDER THE THINGS THAT ARE
OUT OF ORDER AND RAISE AND APPOINT
LEADERS IN EVERY CITY.'
-   Titus 1:5

MICHAEL HUTTON-WOOD MINISTRIES

RELEASING POTENTIAL
- MAXIMIZING DESTINY

HOUSE OF JUDAH (PRAISE) MINISTRIES

&

LEADERS FACTORY INTERNATIONAL

RAISING GENERATIONAL LEADERS
- IMPACTING NATIONS

TABLE OF CONTENTS

INTRODUCTION

When it comes to this subject of marriage, what surprises me is that in life, students who desire to pursue and qualify to practice in certain professions such as medicine (7 years), dentistry (5-7 years), Law (5-7 years), Architecture (3-5 years), Nursing (3-4 years), Engineering (3-5 years), are willing to spend all these years to attend colleges to qualify to practice and continue to do refresher courses while working and retire after a couple of years and yet marriage which is meant to be till death do us part (a lifelong school), most people enter it based on only love or looks and know little or almost nothing at all about it before they enter it.

NO WONDER, THERE ARE SO MANY CASUALTIES.

REMEMBER: IT IS BETTER TO BUILD A FENCE ON TOP OF A CLIFF THAN A HOSPITAL AT THE BOTTOM OF A CLIFF.

This book has been written as a fence-builder to prevent you from becoming one of numerous casualties. Hopefully from this little book, which is the 1st volume and the follow-up to my book, 200 Questions you must ask, investigate and know before you say 'I DO', you will learn a few tips you can practice as an appetizer for the other books coming up to set you on the right track and bring understanding, meaning, breathe life, joy, enjoyment, satisfaction and fulfilment to your marriage.

Marriage is a wonderful thing, and provided we understand it and are prepared to work at it, we can really enjoy it and experience lasting fulfilment.

DE-ICER 1

A FRIEND OF MINE SENT ME THESE EMAILS

HUSBAND SHOPPING STORE

A store that sells husbands has just opened in Windhoek, where a woman may go to choose a husband. Among the instructions at the entrance is a description of how the store operates. You may visit the store **ONLY ONCE!**

There are six floors and the attributes of the men increase as the shopper ascends the flights. There is, however, a catch . . . You may choose any man from a particular floor, or you may choose to go up a floor, but you cannot go back down except to exit the building! So, a woman goes to the Husband Store to find a husband.

On the first floor the sign on the door reads:

Floor 1 - These men have good jobs and love the Lord.

The second floor sign reads:

Floor 2 - These men have good jobs, love the Lord, and love kids.

The third floor sign reads:

Floor 3 - These men have good jobs, love the Lord, they love kids, are very rich and extremely good-looking.

"Wow," she thinks, but feels compelled to keep going. She goes to the fourth floor and sign reads:

The fourth floor sign reads:

Floor 4 - These men have good jobs, love the Lord, love kids, are very rich, good- looking and help with the housework.

"Oh my God" she exclaimed, "I can hardly stand it!" Still, she goes to the fifth floor and sign reads:

Floor 5 - These men have good jobs, love the Lord, love kids, are very rich, gorgeous, help with the housework, and have a strong romantic streak. She is so tempted to stay, but she goes to the sixth floor and the sign reads:

Floor 6 - You are visitor' number 4,363,012 to this floor. There are no men on this floor. This floor exists solely as proof that women are impossible to please. Thank you for shopping at the Husband Store. Watch your step as you exit the building, and have a nice day!

Please send this to all men for a good laugh and to all the women who can handle the truth!

DE-ICER 2:
THE OBEDIENT WIFE

There was a man who had worked hard all his life, had saved all his money, and was a real miser when it came to his money.

Just before he died, he said to his wife....'When I die, I want you to take all my money and put it in the casket with me. I want to take my money to the afterlife with me.'

And so he got his wife to promise him with all of her heart, that when he died, she would put all of the money into the casket with him.

Well, he died. He was stretched out in the casket, his wife was sitting there – dressed in black, and her friend was sitting next to her.

When they finished the ceremony and just before the undertakers got ready to close the casket, the wife said, 'Wait for just a moment!'

She had a small metal box with her; she came over with the box and put it in the casket.

Then the undertakers locked the casket down and they rolled it away.

So her friend said, "Girl, I know you were not foolish

enough to put all that money in there with your husband."

The loyal wife replied, 'Listen, I am a Christian; I cannot go back on my word. I promised him that I was going to put that money into the casket with Him.'

'You mean to tell me you put that money in that casket with him!?!?!?' "I sure did," said the wife. "I got it all together, put it into my account, and wrote him a cheque.......if he can cash it, then he can spend it."

Send this to every clever female you know, and to every man who thinks they are smarter than women!!!

IT

DOESN'T

TAKE

TIME

–

IT

TAKES

TRUTH!

"And in thy majesty ride prosperously because of truth and meekness and righteousness; and thy right hand shall teach thee terrible things." - Psalm 45:4

Chapter One

WHAT IS MARRIAGE?

WHERE PURPOSE IS UNKNOWN

- ABUSE IS INEVITABLE!

21 FACTS ABOUT MARRIAGE:

1. **Marriage: Definition** – As defined by the manual for living (God's Infallible, Unchanging Word – The Holy Bible), it is two people of the opposite sex brought together by God as part of the divine will and purpose of God to live out their lives on this earth based on the teachings of the Holy Scriptures (The Bible).

2. Marriage is the joining together in holy matrimony of a man and a woman who are in love with each other, are convinced they are meant for each other with the intention of building a home together and for the purpose of fulfilling destiny together until death do they part. A healthy "house" and a healthy home is the key to both a

healthy church and a healthy society.

3. The marriage union is the most intimate of all human relationships. For believers it is a union in the Lord. This covenanted union is initiated by God as a provision for the fulfilment, continuation, and edification of mankind which culminates in strong families who then produce strong churches. We all are products of our families, directly as well as indirectly.

4. Marriage is like a precious gem.

5. Marriage is God's idea, not just a good idea. It is only a good idea because it is GOD's idea.

6. Marriage is honourable. Hebrews 13:4 says, 'Marriage is honourable in all, and the bed undefiled: but whoremongers and adulterers God will judge.'

The amplified version says, 'Let marriage be held in honour (esteemed worthy, precious, of great price and especially dear in all things.'

So, it is marriage that is honourable not the people in it. The basic cause of failure in marriage is when people fail to recognize the fact that marriage is honourable not the people in it but marriage itself.

7. **Marriage is an institution.** It is a BLESSED and PERFECT institution and a thing practised on this earth only (Matthew 22:30; Mark 12:25; Luke 20:34-35). For anyone to have a successful marriage they must

understand what marriage really is from God's point of view since He instituted it in the first place. Remember, where purpose is unknown, abuse is inevitable. So, before you encounter the insurmountable, why not go to the Manufacturer and ask some questions which only He can answer! Ask Him to explain to you what He had in mind when He instituted marriage. Seeing it through His eyes will save you all the heartache and frustration that others have been plagued with as a result of ignorance. Marriage is a wonderful thing, and provided we understand it and are prepared to work at it using the prescribed manual, we can really enjoy it and experience lasting fulfilment.

'For he that wanders away from the paths of understanding shall remain in the congregation of then dead.' - Proverbs 21:16

REMEMBER: You are not of the dead, but of the living. So, in all your getting, get understanding of this subject first before you enter this race which has the potential of being the next thing to heaven on earth which if clearly understood before entered into or a life of self-invited and self-inflicted imprisonment with hard labour for the ignorant and jokers.

For Bible says in Proverbs 13:15, 'Good understanding giveth favour: but the way of transgressors [the ignorant] is hard.'

UNDERSTANDING MARRIAGE AS AN INSTITUTION

YOU NEED TO SEE MARRIAGE AS AN INSTITUTION THAT IS HONOURABLE – HIGHLY ESTEEMED, MOST RESPECTACLE.

Scripture says in Proverbs 4:7, 'Wisdom is the principal thing; therefore get wisdom: and with all thy getting get understanding.'

For anyone to have a successful marriage they must understand what marriage really is from God's point of view since He instituted it in the first place. Remember, where purpose is unknown, abuse is inevitable. So, before you encounter the insurmountable, why not go to the manufacturer and ask some questions which only He can answer; ask Him to explain to you what He had in mind when He instituted marriage. Seeing it through His eyes will save you all the heartache and frustration that others have been plagued with as a result of ignorance. I repeat: Marriage is a wonderful thing, and provided we understand it and are prepared to work at it, we will enjoy it and experience lasting fulfilment.

8. Marriage is an institution created by God.

9. Marriage is an institution you enter into not to change it, but to abide by its rules so you can benefit from what it has to offer you, to make you a better person, more effective and prominent, a master at what you do, to graduate with

distinction, increase your salary scale, go into the world and make a great impact in life from what you discovered and applied and eventually recommend it to others.

An institution is something that is established, set, fixed and bigger than one person and it is established before you met it. It was established, instituted before you met it. The following universities and colleges are typical examples of what an institution is: Harvard, Yale, Moorhouse, Regents, Oral Roberts University, (USA) Oxford, Cambridge, Kings College, (UK) Covenant University & Landmark University (Nigeria) Central University College, (Ghana) etc.

So when you enter an institution like the above mentioned, you submit to the institution and the laws that govern it so you can get from it all that you went there for. You take time to discover the times for waking up, your daily schedule, time-table, where the offices and various faculties are located, etc. and you adapt until you graduate from that institution. You don't go there and try to change it to suit your purposes. Similarly, the Bible describes the institution of marriage as one that must be greatly and highly esteemed and respected. It is to be seen as most important, i.e. the institution - not the people in it.

The people in it or the people entering it must see this institution they are entering into as highly esteemed and most important. You submit to it. So, Marriage is a perfect institution for scripture says every good and perfect gift comes from above.

10. So Marriage itself is a perfect institution entered into by two imperfect people, committing themselves to this perfect institution by making perfect vows from imperfect lips. Only God can make this work. That is why you need His manual for successful living containing the wisdom you need which is the principal thing. If you want to see the first imperfect person, look in the mirror.

So, Marriage is two imperfect people, committing themselves to a perfect institution by making perfect vows such as, 'I will never leave you, till death would we part, for better or worse, (better and better - Proverbs 4:18) I'll be there in sickness or in health etc.' but this perfect well-intended vow is coming from imperfect lips.

11. SO MARRIAGE IS PERFECT, IT IS CONSTANT, IT DOES NOT CHANGE; IT IS THE PEOPLE IN IT THAT ARE NOT PERFECT AND ARE CHANGING. SO COMMIT YOURSELF TO SOMETHING THAT DOES NOT CHANGE AND NO MATTER HOW YOU CHANGE, THE THING WILL REMAIN THE SAME FOR YOU. As you live with each other you will discover changes in each of you, in other words you will not remain the same. Both of you will not remain the same forever. Man, the pretty lady you marry today at her age now will not be the one you will live with, in your house. She will be changing all the time and so will you.

YOU DON'T LIVE DAY-TO-DAY WITH THE ONE YOU MARRIED.

Why? Because, they are changing all the time, so are you. So, don't commit yourself to him/her per se but to the institution of marriage that is highly esteemed and must be most respected. Because, you will keep changing, your commitment should be to the institution of marriage so that despite the changes you may see in each other physically, biologically, the age process etc, you will still remain committed to the marriage. For instance, when you join an institution, like a factory, job, college or university, you conform to the set rules laid out there before you joined. You don't go and change the rules to suit your needs or wants or desires. You can make suggestions as to how things can get better but you don't rise up in defiance to change the laid down principles. Principles cannot be changed but methods can and in marriage like an institution, God has laid down certain principles which when you follow, you will get His kind of results.

Violating that will be detrimental to you. When someone upsets or annoys you on the job, you don't just leave that job neither do you resign because you notice that your boss's hair or contemporaries' hair is falling off or the one who sits next to you in the office is going bald, or his/her teeth is falling out or is losing their gorgeous looks, you don't resign from the job and say I am going to look for another job. If you even disagree with them you don't leave that job, you may not speak to them for a little while, but you sort yourself out later on and begin to speak again to each other and so is marriage; you work at relationships till you get it right. The reason why you sort yourselves out and stay on the job is because you consider the institution as more important than your personal feelings so both of you stay on the job.

Another example is when you are undertaking a course and pursuing a degree in an institution like a university and a lecturer or the vice chancellor or a fellow student upsets you real bad, you don't abandon your course or leave that university to look for another one because of that one person's behaviour. You may express your dissatisfaction but you wouldn't stop pursuing your destiny, your future because of that. So changing the institution is not the solution to the problem – just like getting married to someone else will not be the solution to the problem. That is why divorce courts are like taking Paracetamol tablets to cure your chronic migraine. So your commitment to the marriage is your key to success. That is why we must make up our mind that no matter what my wife does to me or my husband does to me, he/she is tripping if they think I will resign because Resignation is divorce. It is not an option because I am not committed to him/her per se but the institution of marriage that I have committed myself to. So the factory does not break down because you quarrelled or were in disagreement with a work colleague. This is not your factory - it is bigger than you so you can't fire people from it. Your attitude should be, 'I don't care what you do to me - you can't get me to resign from you; since we have to work in this office or live and work together in this marriage we might just as well try and get along to make this thing work. Reason being - marriage belongs to God.'

Marriage is an institution - it is constant.

12. Remember, you can't fire anyone from a marriage; it is not yours - it belongs to God, so you can't fire the person. We have been making the people honourable whilst the people are changing forgetting that people in the marriage are changing but marriage itself is constant.

13. Success in marriage does not depend on spouses committing themselves to EACH OTHER as much as it does to their committing themselves to MARRIAGE, the unchanging institution that they have MUTUALLY entered into. Your commitment as long as you remain in that institution is to the institution and so is the marriage [institution]. So, no matter what happens, you are committed to what you committed your life to – the institution of marriage.

14. It's not who you love but what you love – honour and esteem marriage itself.

15. Marriage is a steady unchanging institution entered into by two people who are constantly changing as they grow and mature. Whenever you are entering marriage,

commit yourself to the marriage, not the person, because people – everybody grows and change takes place. If you commit yourself to whoever you marry and think they will remain the same physically, you are deceived.

16. Marriage is bigger than the two people in it.

17. Marriage is two imperfect people committing themselves to a perfect institution, by making perfect vows from imperfect lips.

18. A Happy Marriage is No Accident – it is consciously and deliberately created through the manual, (the Word - Joshua 1:8) continuous nurturing and careful cultivation – you work at it by understanding and engaging what I call THE LOVE COMBINATION ANOINTING [COMBO].

19. Remember: LOVE IS NOT JUST A FEELING, BUT A DISCIPLINE. IT IS A CHOICE.

20. IT TAKES ONLY A FEW MINUTES TO GET MARRIED! BUT BUILDING A MARRIAGE REQUIRES A LIFETIME.

MANY SPEND MORE TIME, RESOURCES AND ENERGY DATING BEFORE MARRIAGE AND STOP DATING AFTER MARRIAGE WHEN IN ACTUAL FACT, DATING SHOUD HAVE CONTINUED AFTER THE WEDDING - in the context of marriage.

I repeat: It takes only a few minutes to get married, but building a marriage requires a lifetime.

21. A GOOD MARRIAGE IS WHAT YOU MAKE IT. Marriage is the next thing to heaven on earth or a hellish life imprisonment on earth with hard labour – you choose!

Deuteronomy 30:19, 'I call heaven and earth to record this day against you, that I have set before you life and death, blessing and cursing: therefore choose life, that both thou and thy seed may live:'

Joshua 24:15, 'And if it seem evil unto you to serve the LORD, choose you this day whom ye will serve; whether the gods which your fathers served that were on the other side of the flood, or the gods of the Amorites, in whose land ye dwell: but as for me and my house, we will serve the LORD.'

Chapter Two

UNDERSTANDING LOVE

"THE GREATEST GIFT A FATHER CAN GIVE TO HIS CHILDREN IS TO LOVE THEIR MOTHER UNCONDITIONALLY"

- Michael Hutton-Wood

LOVE IS AS STRONG AS DEATH!

Song of Solomon 8:6, 'Set me as a seal upon thine heart, as a seal upon thine arm: for love is strong as death; jealousy is cruel as the grave: the coals thereof are coals of fire, which hath a most vehement flame.'

The New Testament was translated from the Greek to

English and from that Greek word, 'LOVE' comes four different meanings as follows:

Bible writers used four different Greek words for Love:

Four Different Meanings of LOVE:

1. Eros - sexual love; from which you get the word erotic; erotic book or shop, erotica; love in order to get something from you; this is physical love; married love; mutual desire between a man and a woman. This is love that is blessed of God and is found in Song of Solomon.

2. Storge (Pronounced storg'ay) – family love. Romans 12:10 says we are to treat Christians like we treat members of our own families – with respect.

3. Phileo (pronounced fil-eh' o) – the love of friendship, the affection we feel for people in friendly relationships. Phileo is a word that has to do with feelings; feelings for people; is a word for friendship love; warm affectionate love of friends; how to be affectionate. Love because of friendship; Phileo also has an element of giving and receiving, an exchange, directly or indirectly.

4. Agape – (pronounced ag-ah' pay) divine love; love in spite of; unconditional love; agape is the kind of love that just gives and gives and gives never really asking for anything in return. That is God's divine kind of love for us which we must have for humanity.

- Agape, however is unselfish. It is the totally unselfish

love of God toward His people; it gives and gives and keeps on giving never really asking for anything in exchange. It is a beautiful concept of love not based on emotions or feelings; it is actually a love by choice, a love that doesn't look for affinity and gives us the ability to love even that which is unlovely, or the unlovable; it always has the best interest of the other person.

GOD DOESN'T CHANCE TO LOVE US - HE CHOOSES TO LOVE US and so must we as Born-Again Christians.

SO, LOVE IS A CHOICE

LOVE IS A DISCIPLINE.

WE CHOOSE TO LOVE IN SPITE OF.

LOVE IS A DECISION.

LOVE IS THE KEY - THE OVERRIDING AND MOTIVATING FORCE.

In the world they say love is blind – in the kingdom, Love is not blind. Love in the kingdom is dead as King Solomon described in Song of Songs 8:6, 'Set me as a seal upon thine heart, as a seal upon thine arm: for love is strong as death; jealousy is cruel as the grave: the coals thereof are coals of fire, which hath a most vehement flame.'

- You are dead to self and alive to God.

In summary:

Agape is the divine love, has the best interest of the other.

Phileo is the love of friendship or brotherly love.

Storge is the love of family.

Eros is the love of man for woman.

QUESTION: What kind of Love do I need in my marriage?

ANSWER: The Kind Of Love Everyone Needs In Order To Have a Successful, Happy, Fruitful, Secure, Sustaining, Satisfying Marriage & Family Life Is - What I Call: COMBO LOVE Or THE LOVE COMBINATION ANOINTING [COMBO].

What I mean by Love Combination Anointing is, all the four kinds of love integrated to work together, hand in hand for fulfilment. This is not an either/or proposition by asking what is your preference or choice such as do you want to choose an affectionate love for people and friends or emotional love based on considerations and the act of the will or loving in spite of. There isn't just a single choice to be made. All of the four kinds of love are involved, are crucial and are an absolute necessity. Let's look at the various combinations and how they work as we deliberately put them together and work them.

SUMMARY:
Agape and eros in a marriage makes it a Christian marriage – an unselfish, thoughtful, loving, considerate marriage union.

Agape and storge in a family makes it a Christian family – a family that is not a civil war or a contest or a volcano ready to erupt or explode, but a family that is solid and strong, a house built on the firm foundation of God's love and His word.

Agape and phileo in a friendship makes it a friendship that is based not on external considerations. It is a friendship that will weather the storms, the adversities, and the setbacks in life – a friendship that will survive no matter how strong the wind is blowing or the earthquakes, or hurricanes of life.

Agape is available in all the relationships of life because Romans 5:5 says it is shed abroad in our hearts by the Holy Ghost.

PRAYER: Pray this prayer of dedication:

'Lord, let my love be as strong as death. I qualify for and have agape (God's kind of love) by redemption. What I need and my marriage relationship, friendship relationships and family relationships need is more of Your agape [unconditional] love, [love inspite of] so I can improve and excel in every relationship I have. Agape will place an unselfish, sacrificial element in my marriage. It will strengthen my family and put solidarity in my friendships to keep them from being exploitative and manipulative. I pray, Lord, that You will empower me to develop Your agape love in me, to make me what you want me to be, so that Your love shows through every area of my life for all to see and benefit from. I thank you for answered prayer in Jesus' Name. Amen.'

THE GRASS IS NOT GREENER ON THE OTHER SIDE.

THE GRASS IS GREENER ONLY WHERE YOU WATER IT.

FIVE KEYS TO STAYING MARRIED TO THE SAME WOMAN

1.

HUSBANDS, FORGIVE YOUR WIVES IN ADVANCE FOR WHAT THEY WILL DO AND SAY AND HOW THEY DO AND SAY IT.

2.

IT'S NOT EVERYTHING YOU SEE, YOU TALK OR COMMENT ON - ZIP YOUR LIP!

3.

NEVER TELL HER SHE'S FAT OR HAS PUT ON WEIGHT! DIPLOMACY! TACT! DIPLOMACY! TACT! APPLY ALL!

4.

WHEN SHE'S UPSET AND WANTS TO TALK, AND CALLS YOU INTO 'CONFERENCE', NEVER SAY, 'WHAT IS IT

THIS TIME?' TRUST ME ON THIS!

5.

WHEN YOU GET A CALL FROM HER ASKING, 'ARE YOU DRIVING?' CONFESS ALL YOUR KNOWN AND UNKNOWN 'SINS' TO GOD WHETHER YOU HAVE ONE OR NOT AND MAKE SURE YOU ARRIVE AT THE 'CONFERENCE' CENTRE EARLY AND LOWER YOUR DEFENCES; – THE 'CONFERENCE' WILL FINISH QUICKER!

GRACE! GRACE! GRACE!

Chapter Three

101 TIPS FOR A GREAT MARRIAGE

This section contains 101 tips for a good, solid, exciting, spicy, enjoyable, creative, loving, innovative, happy, joyful, lasting, fulfilling, emulative & exemplary marriage broken down under five [5] categories:

1. First things first: Gratitude, prayer and the Word

2. Love and romantic matters - Celebrating your together moments

3. General Matters

4. What to be - Do's and Don'ts – Never Do's

5. Sexual Matters

SCRIPTURAL BASIS:

Genesis 2:18, 'And the LORD God said, It is not good that the man should be alone; I will make him an help meet for him.'

Genesis 2:21-24, 'And the LORD God caused a deep sleep to fall upon Adam, and he slept: and he took one of his ribs, and closed up the flesh instead thereof; And the rib, which the LORD God had taken from man, made he a woman, and brought her unto the man. And Adam said, This is now bone of my bones, and flesh of my flesh: she shall be called Woman, because she was taken out of Man. Therefore shall a man leave his father and his mother, and shall cleave unto his wife: and they shall be one flesh.'

TO THE MARRIED I GIVE THIS COMMAND – 1 Corinthians 7:10, 'And unto the married I command, yet not I, but the Lord, Let not the wife depart from her husband:'

Ephesians 5:25, 'Husbands, love your wives, even as Christ also loved the church, and gave himself for it;'

Colossians 3:19, 'Husbands, love your wives, and be not bitter against them.'

FIRST THINGS FIRST - GRATITUDE, PRAYER AND THE WORD:

1. Start each day with gratitude, praise, prayer and thanksgiving to God and a hug, a peck or kiss for

your spouse.

2.   Pray for each other daily and enjoy the word every blessed moment. That is the stability of your time.

3.   Compromise in every area except for God's Word.

LOVE AND ROMANTIC MATTERS:

4.   Touch each other often and gently.

5.   Give back rubs.

6.   Select a song and make it "our song".

7.   Watch sunsets together.

8.   Cuddle. (Just cuddle)

9.   Fix their breakfast - Bring each other breakfast in bed occasionally.

10. Go on walks and romantic outings together.

11. Hold hands in public.

12. Talk about your love for each other.

13. Ask, 'what can I do to make you happier' – always put the other person's interest above yours.

14. Give gifts to each other sacrificially.

15.   Give advice in a loving way when asked for.

16. Take time to notice, acknowledge, and express love for and honest appreciation of each other on a daily basis and what you do for each other.

17. Pay "little attentions" – be proactive in giving attention to your spouse – it will help keep romance and the spirit of courtship alive in the relationship, even after many years of marriage.

18. Put your hand on her thighs occasionally while driving, (obviously keep your eyes on the road) rub it gently and leave it there for a few seconds; it's an expression or sign of assurance that you love her, you care and are there for her; it's also an assurance that it is well or it will be well.

19. TREATMENT: Treat each other the way you treat your best client; never treat anyone else better than your spouse – serve them from your heart – it can be seen.

20. Cultivate intimacy. Leave and cleave! Be hooked up for the journey, whatever it takes. You cannot make it on your own.

21. Smile and Wink at each other (across the room if you are not sitting together).

22. Date your spouse at least once a week. It strengthens intimacy, boosts your friendship and bonds you together.

23. Reminisce about your favourite times together. Go

down [pleasant] memory lane.

24. Celebrate birthdays in a big way.

25. Send flowers and if possible a gift every Valentine's Day, birthday, anniversary, mothers' day and for no reason at all.

26. Set up a romantic get-away.

27. Occasionally run her a bath while you do the dishes and put the children to bed. Then you can join her and bathe together by scrubbing her body first. [Keep scoring points – she will cash it in for you]

28. Write each other a letter occasionally, expressing how much you love and are proud of each other and buy cards that expresses your undying and ever-increasing love and appreciation for each other, put it in the post [name and all] to arrive at your address. [Surprise, surprise]

29. Send a card for no reason - Surprise your spouse with a card, flowers or gift including money.

30. Sometimes when your wife brings your meal in a tray with the full service, surprise her by placing some money under the plate as 'keepers and finders' for her. [You know the next meal will come with full service, right!]

31. No matter what happens, wear your wedding ring.

32. Pay Compliments to each other at least twice a day. Definitely notice and pay compliments to your wife when she dresses up at home before you compliment others outside or your 'neck' and 'dinner' will be on the line.

33. Call her on the phone during the day and make full use of modern technology [such as sending romantic and other text messages from your mobile phone or e-mail messages where applicable].

34. Consciously and genuinely let your face light up every time your spouse walks into the room wherever you are.

GENERAL MATTERS:

35. Accept your differences.

36. Smile often.

37. 'Chillax' (chill and relax).

38. Laugh together. Laughter must be present always. Have or develop a sense of humour; even God has a sense of Humour. (Psalm 2) Find things to laugh about together.

39. Talk about your dreams and aspirations and assist each other side by side to fulfil their purpose here on earth.

40. Do what the other person wants before they ask.

41. Do it their way.

42. Listen carefully. [A must]

43. Know their needs and meet them.

44. Admire your spouse.

45. Respect each other.

46. Encourage each other.

47. Try to look your best always even at home.

48. Apologise.

49. Forgive quickly.

50. Respond quickly to the other person's requests.

51. Find ways to surprise and delight your spouse with "RANDOM ACTS OF THOUGHTFULNESS."

52. Neglect the whole world rather than one another.

53. Prefer each other over others.

54. Slow down - pace yourself for the long journey.

55. Show unparalleled respect for each other by asking for the other's opinion.

56. Treat each other's friends and relatives with courtesy.

BE:

57. Be the wise Bamboo.

58. Be optimistic – it will definitely work as you work at it.

59. Be best friends; the two of you should be each other's best friend, operate as one unit and defend as one unit.

60. Be courteous - Always show courtesy.

61. Be kind.

62. Be vulnerable. (Open)

63. Be polite.

64. Be gentle.

65. Be positive

66. Be selfless.

67. Be generous to each other.

68. Be spontaneous – do something unexpected for the other's benefit.

DO's AND DON'Ts - Don't or do not:

69.   Don't get too familiar or over familiar – don't take each other for granted - it breeds contempt.

70.   Don't allow anyone to meddle in your affairs. Give your family privacy especially if you are a Pastor or Minister or have a public ministry or are under the gaze of the media. Seek confidential outside help within your spiritual family tree only when desperately needed.

71.   Do not discuss only work-related matters with your partner. Adopt and keep an open and honest communication with your spouse on all matters except on confidential matters relating to work or what you know will disturb him/her.

72.   Don't assume your spouse is dumb or stupid or cannot comprehend or handle certain information when teaching her. Take time for just the two of you to sit down and talk calmly and discuss openly about everything. This will make your journey a whole lot easier. Communication is a discipline.

73.   Don't ever assume love – love needs to be expressed regularly and often and in different ways – it should never be assumed.

- Husband, never assume your wife knows you love her - tell her.

- Wife, never assume your husband knows you love him - tell him.

- Love may indeed "Spring eternal" but our expression of it needs to be refreshed each day in various ways.

- Say, 'I love you' to each other frequently and show it in different ways.

- At least once every day, try to say one kind complimentary word to your partner.

74. On the subject of communication, don't assume you know each other's needs. Consciously, make sure you study to know and understand each other's needs. Men have a conquering problem-solving spirit. However, let your husband know that sometimes when you have an issue, or are quiet, you just want him to be there to listen and not necessarily offer a solution or attempt to solve any problem. Just be there, honey; that's all I need.

75. In the pursuit of your careers, professions, callings or ministry, **complete each other; don't compete with each other.** Never envy the progress, acceleration or success of your spouse especially your wife even if she earns more than you. Your attitude should be: Hey, it's our money.

NEVER:

76. Never be angry at the same time.

77. Never yell at each other except the house is on fire.

78. Never go to sleep with an argument unsettled.

79. Never bring up mistakes of the past. Never keep record of wrongs.

80. Never attempt to win any argument - this is not a competition. If one of you has to win an argument, let it be the other one.

81. Never criticise judgmentally but constructively. If you have to criticize, do it lovingly.

82. Never insist on pulling out of your husband what is on his mind by force when he's in deep thought. A wife must understand that her husband cannot always tell her what is on his mind at the time she asked. It may not be helpful.

83. Never assume you know your husband. Rather, consciously take time to study him as they study you as the Bible advocates: dwell with your wives according to knowledge:

- Always remember the following about men, especially your husband:

- Men do not talk (they internalise, and then they talk

when the matter is resolved within).

- Men process thoughts internally (women process thoughts externally/verbally).

- Men consider all options, and then conclude firmly. Information being processed is no good for the wife (who will be affected by it). When conclusions have been arrived at; then the wife should be told.

84. Never have a loose tongue. Both of you should be keepers and wise custodians of secrets. Badly-handled secrets will condition your partner never to share secrets or talk about personal matters again (even if they don't say so).

85. Never criticise or demean your spouse in public, to friends, family, relatives or anyone. Defend your spouse to others both in private and in public i.e. in their presence and in their absence. Brag about your spouse to other people behind their back, i.e. in their absence.

86. Never allow money to be your master but your servant. When it comes to Money – Enjoy it now, use it as a servant, not your master and then pass it on. (Be addicted to giving, generosity and liberality)

87. Never be proud. Pride leads to a fall. Rather, make your boast in the Lord; let your pride emanate from the fact and truth that, you are in Christ.

88. Never put pressure on your spouse to change publicly, privately or in your prayer chamber. Change together – Grow gracefully old together.

89. Never take on a defensive posture when you have done something wrong. Rather be ready to admit you are wrong and ask for forgiveness. It portrays humility, meekness and builds respect.

90. Never forget any major milestone in your partner's life. Always celebrate your marriage and other occasions dear to your spouse remembering that he/she who is married will care for the things of the world.

91. Never hide your bank statements, bank account details, your salary or your monetary affairs from your spouse. If he or she is a spendthrift then mention it, discuss it, educate him/her and put things in place that the future is not squandered away through indiscipline, greed, selfishness or mismanagement. Learn and practice 'delayed gratification'. Spouses should compliment (and not conflict).

92. Never make your disagreements public. Marriage has winding roads (try not to make it public). Remember, people are people (with strengths and weaknesses) including you. [Never use derogatory words against your spouse such as calling your wife or husband an idiot or a fool. No, you will be considered a bigger idiot or bigger fool to have

chosen, dated, engaged, spent good money to marry an idiot and a fool, with your eyes wide open.]

93. Never keep important matters and must-knows from your spouse. Update periodically with changes within/without) - it creates peace, trust, confidence, assurance and harmony at home.

94. Never start your marriage insisting on maintaining your personal single accounts only. Operate a joint account and apply the 80/20% or 75/25% principle where the joint account is reserved for the majors and the 20/25% shared between both of you to be used for the minors - your personal needs/wants. Remember: HIS MONEY IS YOUR MONEY AND HER MONEY IS YOUR MONEY within reason. [The two are one]

95. Never drive past your own house more than once. Make it easy for each other to come back home. Never step out of the house after an argument – you may be cornering trouble for yourself without knowing!

96. Stop trying to make your spouse fit into your definitions and expectations. Encourage each other to maximise your destinies and fulfil your individual callings and assignments together.

97. Never allow your love for each other to grow cold. Develop your love for each other to become as

strong as death (Song of Solomon 8:6). Love is the major currency you trade and the greatest motivator in all you do.

98.   Don't maintain habits that cause strife and division at home. Get rid of habits that annoy or upset your spouse.

SEXUAL MATTERS:

Selfless actions or behaviours which enhance romance and love-making i.e. SEX in marriage.

99.   Prioritise your sex life.

- Don't leave it to chance or your spouse - plan for it.

- Be inventive.

- Be creative.

- Be innovative.

- Add spice and life.

- Invent new things to give it life and vibrancy always.

- Rub her feet and give her massages.

- Be sensitive, aware and responsive to each other's sexual needs and desires.

- Be open to new ideas and suggestions that will enhance your sex life including healthy books, CDs, DVDs, etc.

- It is very important that husbands and wives especially wives, learn to speak up regarding their sexual needs – these may sound like small things but they are the things that will keep the fire burning in a marriage. It's the little fixes that spoil the vine and the same other little additions that spark and adds to the enjoyment leading to satisfaction.

- Don't forget the little things – they matter and are the building blocks for the big things - Songs of Solomon 2:15.

- Ultimate success in everything depends to a great deal on giving attention to little things as much as the great things including romance and sex.

REMEMBER:

- Sex begins in the kitchen, I.e. Husband, don't sit there watching TV and changing channels all day expecting manifestations at night when you've left her to do all the house chores and she's worn out and say you will meet her upstairs. You'll wait till the second coming of Christ. Rather, if you don't want her to lie down like a timber [which you complain about] while you just come and take as may be your habit, then, assist her with the house chores so she's not worn out before you make love [have sex]. That way both of you are energized, actively involved, refreshed, satisfied and fulfilled.

- Sex is not a side issue with God – it is part of the marriage covenant.

- Sex is not love but an outward expression or demonstration of love.

- Sex is not spiritual.

- Sex is 100 percent physical and chemical.

- Sex is a spiritual union between two married people – a joining of spirit to spirit - a coupling of two people – a joining of flesh to flesh.

- Sex is an appetite God built into us when He created us; God designed us for appetites – you can call it cravings, drives, hungers, passions, whatever - it is still appetites.

- Sex is also for procreation – Genesis 1:28.

- Sex with our spouse is for recreation and release - it is for sheer joy and the pleasure it affords married couples.

- Sex is fun - God meant for us to enjoy sex; otherwise why would He have designed it to be so pleasurable?

- Sex is for communication – it is a loving environment that encourages communication, sexual consummation and provides an intimacy and communion that goes far beyond words.

- Sexual activity is restricted to marriage.

- Sexual relations are a normal part of a marriage - each spouse has the right to expect from the other as well as the responsibility to give to the other (1 Corinthians 7:3-5).

- Sexual fulfilment and happiness in marriage depends on an open, loving, accepting and affirming environment in which each spouse feels comfortable making his or her needs and desires known to each other.

- Concerning sexual behaviour: The question is not what we can get from each other but what we can give to each other and it is not about we can get away with, but what is healthy and edifying.

- Whatever we can do and be edified and not feel guilty afterwards is lawful and appropriate; if it does not edify, it is inappropriate.

- Discover from each other what satisfies each other i.e. your spouse and within healthy ethical boundaries and your faith, enjoy yourselves and satisfy each other.

- With sex, look good and fresh always.

- Look forward to making love to each other with eager, joyful, exciting anticipation.

- Be creative, innovative with the music, candles, lights and in setting up the right atmosphere and conducive environment.

- Defraud not each other.

- Don't put a timetable or unreasonable restrictions on satisfying each other sexually.

- Remember the triangle and trapezium mentality and orientation of men and women so you don't leave the other dissatisfied - men are like triangles when it comes to sex - they look, admire, desire their woman and reach their climax and peak quicker but women require processing to reach a certain dimension before they can reach their peak/climax, hence what is called foreplay involving kissing, touching the sensitive parts for arousal before penetration. These are all pre-requisites that must be borne in mind and consciously worked at so no one is left dissatisfied.

- As much as possible both of you should discuss, study, work at and know what arouses you and deliberately and consciously work at doing it willingly and joyfully reaching your climax together or within close proximity of each other so both are satisfied and none is left wanting, feeling cheated or dissatisfied.

IN CLOSING:

100. Welcome each other home with expectation, eagerness, excitement and occasional surprises.

101. End each day with prayer, thanksgiving, praise to God and a hug, a peck, a kiss or a cuddle for your

spouse - if it leads to the bonus of you 'knowing each other scripturally' like Adam did with Eve, PRAISE GOD and if not, still PRAISE GOD!

NOTES:

THE GREATEST GIFT

If you want to take advantage of the contents of this message by asking God to give you power to lead, from which Adam fell, you need to give your life to Jesus Christ. If you have never met or experienced a definite encounter with Jesus Christ, you can know Him today. You can make your life right with Him by accepting Him as your personal Lord and Saviour by praying the following prayer out loud where you are. Pray this prayer with me now:

PRAYER FOR SALVATION: 'O God, I ask you to forgive me for my sins. I believe You sent Jesus to die on the cross for me and confess it with my mouth. I receive Jesus Christ as my personal Lord and Saviour and confess Him as Lord of my life and I give my life willingly to Him now. Thank you Lord for saving me and for making me a new person in Jesus' Name, (2 Corinthians 5:17) Amen.'

If you prayed this prayer, you have now become a child of God (John 1:12) and I welcome you to the family of God. Please let me know about your decision for Jesus by writing to me. I would like to send you some free literature to help you in your new walk with the Lord. So please write to me at the following address:

Correspondence address:

Michael Hutton-Wood,

House of Judah (Praise) Ministries

P. O. Box 1226,

Croydon. CR9 6DG. UK.

Or call:

Within the UK:

0208 689 6010, 07956 815 714

Outside the UK:

+44 208 689 6010, +44 7956 815 714

Alternatively Email us at:

Email: info@houseofjudah.org.uk

michaelhutton-wood@fsmail.net

Or visit us at: Website: www.houseofjudah.org.uk

Watch our 24hour internet TV experience on www.judahtv.org

OTHER BOOKS AND LEADERSHIP MANUALS BY AUTHOR

1. A Must For Every New Convert

2. You Need To Do The Ridiculous In Order To Experience The Miraculous

3. 175 Reasons Why You Cannot And Will Not Fail In Life

4. What To Do In The Darkest Hour Of Your Trial [125 Bible Truths You Must Know, BELIEVE, REMEMBER, CONFESS AND DO]

5. Why You should Pray And How You should Pray For Your Pastor and Your Church Daily

6. 200 Questions You Must Ask, Investigate And Know Before You Say 'I Do'

7. I Shall Rise Again

8. How to negotiate your desired future with today's currency

9. Leadership Secrets

10. Leadership Nuggets

11. Leadership Capsules

12. Success is by choice and failure is by choice

13. The Dangers of Procrastination

14. Wisdom Bank

Training Manuals For Impactful Leadership & Effective Ministry

Academy 101 [House Of Judah Academy Curriculum]

Ministry 101

Leadership 101

Kingdom Prosperity 101 From School Of Kingdom Prosperity & Financial Management

Pastoral Leadership 101 From School Of Impactful Pastoral Leadership

Prescriptions For Fulfilling Your Ministry

To order copies of any of these books, ministry or leadership manuals or for a product catalog of other literature, audiotapes and CDs, DVDs, write to:

Michael Hutton-Wood Ministries, P. O. Box 1226, Croydon. CR9 6DG. UK. or [in the UK call] - 0208 689 6010; [outside UK call] + 442086896010

You can also place your order online as you visit our website: www.houseofjudah.org.uk

You can also email us at: Email: info@houseofjudah.org.uk; or michaelhutton-wood@fsmail.net

Global Initiatives And Ministries Within The Ministry

TV MINISTRY IN THE UK

Watch Leadership Secrets on KICC TV
SKY Channel 594

Tuesday & Thursday – 3pm & Saturday 5.30pm

Monday-Friday 2pm on FAITH TV
Sky channel 593 & Saturday 3.30pm

LOG ON AND WATCH OUR INTERNET TV PROGRAM on WWW.JUDAHTV.ORG

Anytime - anywhere.

Featuring the:

Teaching Channel
Motivation Channel
Leadership Channel
Family/ Relationships Channel
Upcoming Events/ Products

WATCH US ON YouTube and AUDIO
STREAMING EVERY WEEK
@ www.houseofjudah.org.uk

Partnering With A Global Ministry Within A Ministry

Michael Hutton-Wood Ministries (The HUTTON-WOOD WORLD OUTREACH MINISTRY) is the apostolic, missions, world outreach, and evangelistic wing of the House of Judah (Praise) Ministries with a mission to God's end time church and the nations of the earth. This ministry was born out of a strong God-given mandate to reach, touch and impact the nations of the earth with the gospel of Christ and bring back divine order, discipline, integrity, godly character, excellence and stability to God's people and God's house. It has a strong apostolic mandate to set in order the things that are out of order and lacking in the church [The Body of Christ] – (Titus 1:5).

Its mission is to save the lost at any cost, depopulate hell and populate heaven with souls that have experienced in full, the new birth, renewal of mind, to produce believers walking in the fullness of their Godly inheritance, divine health, prosperity and authority to take their homes, communities, cities and nations for Christ and occupy till Christ returns. It is to raise a people without spot, wrinkle or blemish. The man of God's passion and drive is that as truly as he lives, this earth shall be filled with the knowledge of the glory of the Lord as the waters cover the sea. His determination is not to rest, hold back or keep silent until he sees the body of Christ established as a praise in the earth. (Numbers 14:21; Habakkuk 2:14; Isaiah 62:6-7)

If you would like to join the faithful brethren and partners of this great ministry by becoming a partner as we believe God for ten thousand partners to partner with this vision prayerfully and financially, ask for a copy of the partners' club commitment card by writing to:

Michael Hutton-Wood Ministries

[Hutton-Wood World Outreach]

P. O. Box 1226, Croydon. Surrey.

CR9 6DG. UK.

Alternatively, you can send a monthly contribution by cheque payable to our ministry or donate online at www. houseofjudah.org.uk or request a direct debit mandate or standing order form from your bankers or us made payable to Michael Hutton-Wood Ministries. Call +44 [0] 208 689 6010 for more details. Philippians 4:19 be your portion and experience as you partner with this work and global mandate. Shalom!

Generational Leadership Training Institute

(The Leaders' Factory)

The Mandate: Raising Generational Leaders, Impacting Nations.

The Generational Leadership Training Institute (GLTI) is the Leadership training and mentoring wing of our ministry with a global mandate to raise leaders with a generational thinking mindset, not a now mentality and to fulfil the Law of Explosive Growth – To add growth, lead followers – To multiply, lead leaders.

This is a Bible College, Leadership Training Institute fulfilling the Matthew 9:37-38 mandate of developing and releasing labourers for the end time harvest. We offer fulltime and part time certificate, diploma, degree and short twelve-week courses in biblical studies, counselling, leadership, practical ministry and schools of prosperity. Its aim is to raise leaders who know and live not just by the anointing but by ministerial ethics, leaders who build with a long term mentality, who live today with tomorrow in mind. The mission of this unique educational and impartation institution is to transform followers into generational leaders and its motto is to raise leaders of discipline, integrity, godly character and excellence - D.I.C.E.

For correspondence, full time, part time, online courses, prospectus, fees and registration forms for the next course, call 0208 689 6010 or write to the Registrar, GLTI, P. O. Box 1226, Croydon. CR9 6DG. UK or from outside UK call +44 208 689 6010.

Additional information can be obtained from visiting our website www.houseofjudah.org.uk looking for THE LEADERS FACTORY.

Log on to www.judahtv.org for Leadership Secrets and other teaching.

This is a hutton-wood publication

LEADERS FACTORY INTERNATIONAL

MANDATE: 'In the business of training, developing and raising and releasing more leaders and leaders of leaders.'

'Leaders must be close enough to relate to others, but far enough ahead to motivate them.' – John Maxwell

'You must live with people to know their problems, and live with God in order to solve them.' – P. T. Forsyth

If you, your organisation, college, university, business or church would like to invite Dr. Michael Hutton-Wood for a Motivational-speaking, mentoring or leadership coaching engagement or to organize or hold a Leaders Factory seminar or conference, Leadership Development or Human Capital building seminar, Emerging leaders seminar, Management seminar, Business seminar, Effective people-management, Wealth-creation seminar or training for your workers, leaders, staff, ministers, employers, employees, congregation, youth, etc. you can contact us on 0208 689 6010 [UK] +44208 689 6010 [OUTSIDE UK].

Alternatively by email at:

- info@houseofjudah.org.uk

- michaelhutton-wood@fsmail.net

or leadersfactoryinternational@yahoo.com

VISIT our website: www.houseofjudah.org.uk

You can watch our internet TV experience www. judahtv.org [Maximizing Destiny and Leadership Secrets].

This is a Hutton-Wood publication

MANDATE:

Releasing Potential - Maximizing Destiny

Raising Generational Leaders - Impacting Nations

SIMPA
SCEPTRE INTERNATIONAL MINISTERS & PASTORS ASSOCIATION

This covenant mandate comes from Genesis 49:10: 'The sceptre [of Leadership] shall not depart from JUDAH, nor a lawgiver from between his feet, until Shiloh come and unto Him shall the gathering of the people be'

Other covenant scriptures backing this mandate are: Isaiah 55:4 & Titus 1:5. We have a leadership assignment to RAISE GENERATIONAL LEADERS TO IMPACT NATIONS BY DISCOVERING MEN/WOMEN AND EMPOWERING THEM TO RELEASE THEIR POTENTIAL TO MAXIMIZE THEIR DESTINY.

SIMPA is a multi-cultural fellowship/network of diverse Christian leaders, pastors and ministers that recognize the need for fathering, covering and mentoring. The heartbeat of the man of God is to pour into the willing and obedient what has made him and keeps making him from what he's learnt from his father in the Lord, his teachers and mentors which is working for him and producing maximally. He said: 'I discovered this secret early: Not to learn from or follow those who make promises but from those who have obtained the promises, proofs and results. REMEMBER: YOU DON'T NEED TO MAKE NOISE TO MAKE NEWS. SO: FOLLOW NEWS-MAKERS NOT NOISE-MAKERS!'

These are a few of the mindsets of the man of God:

When the students are ready, the teacher will teach.

'YOU NEED FATHERS TO FATHER YOU TO GROW FEATHERS TO FLY.' – Bishop Oyedepo

'Without a father to father you, you can never grow feathers to fly and go further in life, than they went and accomplish more than they did.' – Michael Hutton-Wood

Don't raise money; raise men and you'll have all the money you need to accomplish your assignment.

There is no new thing under the sun – King Solomon

What you desire to attain, become and accomplish in life, someone has accomplished it – find them, follow them, learn from them, sow into them and their resource materials and you will do more than they did and get there faster.

Teachers, Trainers, Mentors and Fathers give you speed/acceleration in every field of endeavour.

Isaac Newton is known to have said the following:

'If I have seen further it has been by standing on the shoulders of those who have gone ahead of me.'

Variant translations: 'Plato is my friend, Aristotle is my friend, but my best friend is truth.'

'Plato is my friend — Aristotle is my friend — truth is a greater friend.'

'If I have seen further it is only by standing on the shoulders of giants.'

Without a reference you can never become a reference.

If you don't refer to anyone no one will refer to you.

Who laid / lays hands on you and what did / do they leave behind?

This is not a money-making venture but rather about covering and empowerment for fulfilment of destiny and assignment within time allocated.

The goal of SIMPA is to spiritually cover, strengthen, equip, empower, train, mentor and encourage and lift up the arms/hands of both emerging and active [full and part time] pastors, ministers and leaders and by so doing release them to fulfil their respective assignments both in ministry and the market place.

IF YOU WOULD LIKE TO BE A PART OF SIMPA, ASK FOR A REGISTRATION FORM & PAMPHLET FROM OUR INFORMATION DESK in House of Judah or email info@houseofjudah.org.uk or call [in the UK] 0208 689 6010 [outside UK call] + 44 208 689 6010 requesting for SIMPA registration form and pamphlet.

– SEE YOU ON TOP!

Shalom! – Bishop

PARTNERSHIP:

In the UK write or send cheque donations to:
Michael Hutton-Wood Ministries
P. O. Box 1226
Croydon. CR9 6DG. UK.

In the UK Call: 0208 689 6010; 07956 815 714
Outside the UK call: +44 208 689 6010;
+ 44 7956 815 714
Fax: +44 20 8689 3301
Email:
info@houseofjudah.org.uk
michaelhutton-wood@fsmail.net
leadersfactoryinternational@yahoo.com
judah@houseofjudah.freeserve.co.uk

Or visit or donate online at our secure
WEBSITE: www.houseofjudah.org.uk

Watch our 24 hour internet TV experience by logging
on anywhere - anytime @ www.judahtv.org

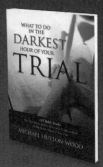

OTHER BOOKS BY THE AUTHOR
- BISHOP MICHAEL HUTTON-WOOD -

Why You Should Pray for your
Pastor And For Your Church Daily

200 Questions You Must Ask, Investigate
And Know Before You Say I Do

A Must For Every New Convert

How To Negotiate Your Desired
Future With Today's Currency

Leadership Secrets

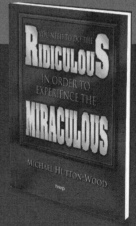

You Need To Do The Ridiculous
In Order To Experience The Miraculous

Please log on to
www.houseofjudah.org.uk for more information